HOW TO SURVIVE IN SPACE

Ruth Owen

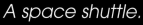

A space shuttle.

Publisher: Melissa Fairley
Art Director: Faith Booker
Editor: Emma Dods
Designer: Emma Randall
Production Controller: Ed Green
Production Manager: Suzy Kelly

Copyright © TickTock Entertainment Ltd 2010

First published in Great Britain in 2010 by TickTock Entertainment Ltd,
The Old Sawmill, 103 Goods Station Road, Tunbridge Wells, Kent, TN1 2DP

ISBN: 978 1 84898 214 7

Printed in China
1 3 5 7 9 10 8 6 4 2

Picture credits (t=top; b=bottom; c=centre; l=left; r=right; OFC=outside front cover; OBC=outside back cover):
NASA/Courtesy of nasaimages.org.: 1, 2, 4, 5, 8, 9, 10, 12–13, 15, 16, 17, 18, 19 (both), 20, 21, 22–23, 24–25, 25t,
26, 27, 31. Science Photo Library: 14. Shutterstock: OFC (all), 6c, 6–7, OBC (all). www.janespencer.com: 11, 28–29.

Thank you to Lorraine Petersen and the members of _nasen._

Every effort has been made to trace copyright holders, and we apologize in advance for any omissions.
We would be pleased to insert the appropriate acknowledgements in any subsequent edition of this publication.

NOTE TO READERS
The website addresses are correct at the time of publishing. However, due to the ever-changing
nature of the Internet, websites and content may change. Some websites can contain links that
are unsuitable for children. The publisher is not responsible for changes in content or website
addresses. We advise that Internet searches should be supervised by an adult.

CONTENTS

An astronaut during a space walk.

CHAPTER 1

SPACE AND THE HUMAN BODY

Have you ever wondered what it is like to go into space?

What is it like to live on a space station 350 kilometres above the Earth?

Space shuttle launch

Astronauts have to travel, live and work in an extreme environment. The human body was not designed to survive in this environment.

There is no air to breathe in space. It is so cold that the human body would freeze. Harmful rays from the Sun would burn human skin.

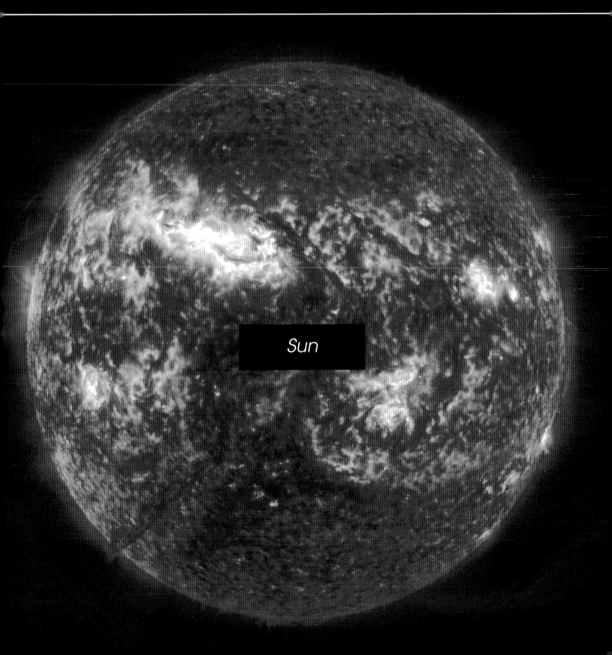

Sun

If you left a spacecraft without a spacesuit, you would pass out in just a few seconds. You would be dead within a minute or two.

Without air, there is no oxygen. People need to breathe oxygen all the time, or they die.

On Earth, air pressure provides a force on our bodies. In space, there is no air pressure. This means the pressure inside your body would push outward. However, there would be no outside force pushing back to balance it.

The gases in your organs would expand quickly. Your organs would swell up. Your body would become swollen. Blood would no longer be able to go round your body.

To survive in space, astronauts must use special clothing and equipment. They must also train hard.

Could you be an astronaut?

Do you have what it takes...
...to survive in space?

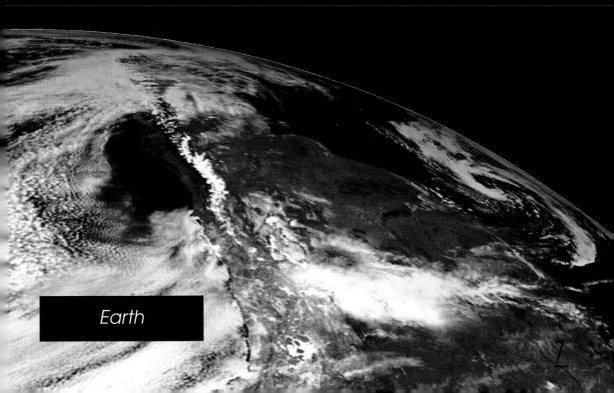

Earth

7

CHAPTER 2

TRAINING FOR SPACE SURVIVAL

Astronauts are trained to be experts at space survival.

As a NASA astronaut candidate you will take part in a one-year course. You will learn how to fly and repair spacecraft. If something goes wrong on a spacecraft, it is up to you and your crew to fix it!

An astronaut during a spacecraft training session

You will also have medical training. If an astronaut is hurt or gets ill in space, the other crew members must know what to do.

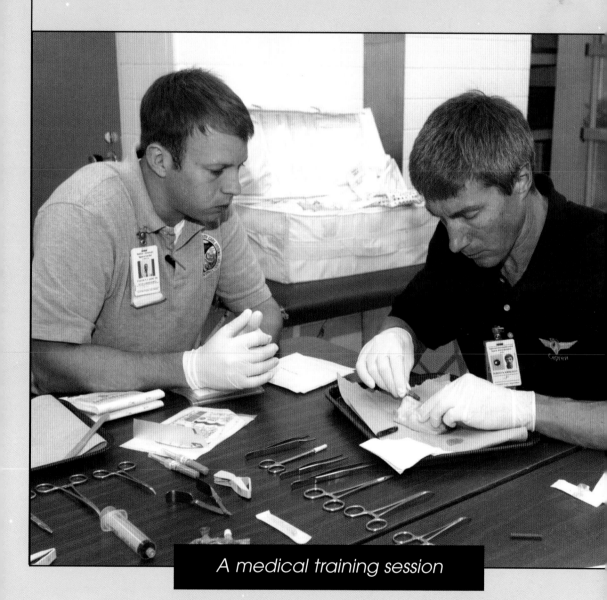

A medical training session

CHAPTER 3

SPACESUITS FOR SURVIVAL

Sometimes, you will have to leave the safety of your spacecraft. This is called a space walk, or EVA (Extra-Vehicular Activity).

You will need to wear a spacesuit to protect you from the extreme environment in space.

An astronaut during an EVA

A spacesuit is like a small spacecraft. The spacesuit has 14 different layers.

LCVG (Liquid Cooling Ventilation Garment) keeps your body cool. It has three layers that draw away your sweat and carry cool water.

Bladder layer (keeps air pressure at the right level and holds in oxygen for breathing)

Seven layers of insulation to protect you from heat and cold

Layer to keep bladder layer in place

The outer layer is made of materials that can resist water, fire and even bullets.

Tear-resistant layer

An important part of the spacesuit is
the helmet. This gives you oxygen.

The helmet's visor is covered in a thin layer of gold.
The gold protects you from the Sun's harmful rays.

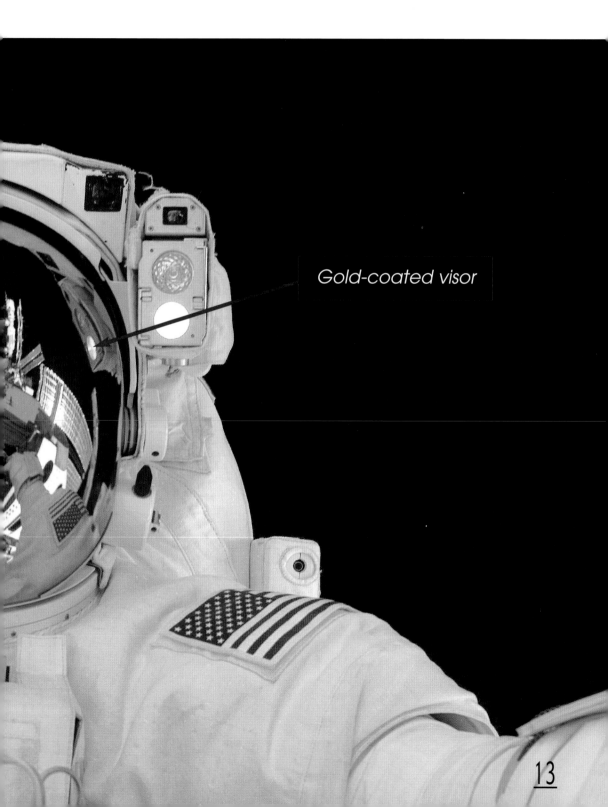

Gold-coated visor

At NASA there are lots of different-sized spacesuit parts.

A variety of spacesuit sizes

Scientists will take measurements all over your body. The measurements will be compared to all the spacesuit parts at NASA. Then, the scientists will build a suit for you. It will fit you perfectly.

Checking the fit of a spacesuit

CHAPTER 4

SURVIVING SPACE WALKS

Astronauts make space walks to build or repair the International Space Station (ISS).

A space walk to repair the ISS

During a space walk, you might be out in space fo
a long time. You could not survive without a space

During a space walk, you will wear a backpack ca
a Primary Life-Support Subsystem (PLSS). The PLSS h
oxygen tanks. It also removes the harmful carbon
dioxide that you breathe out.

PLSS

During a space walk, you will wear safety tethers. The safety tethers stop you floating off into space.

Safety tethers

You will also wear a piece of flying equipment called SAFER (Simplified Aid for EVA Rescue). SAFER is powered by small jet thrusters. If your tether breaks, you can fly back to the spacecraft. You will use a joystick to steer SAFER.

PLSS

SAFER

Gas supply for thrusters

Joystick

Untethered astronaut testing the SAFER

**Each mission or space walk is different.
If you make a mistake, the mission
could fail. You might even be killed.**

You might be chosen to go on a space
walk to fix the Hubble Space Telescope.

During the space walk, you will be floating.
This is because there is no gravity in space.

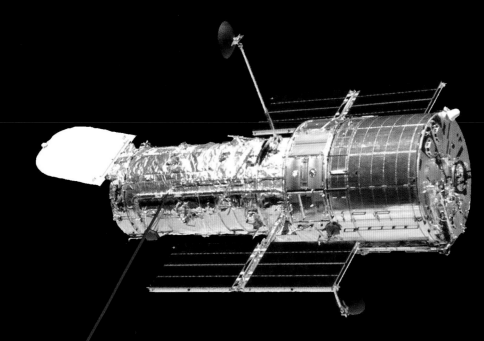

Hubble Space Telescope

You will have to carry out difficult engineering tasks.
This will be very difficult when you are floating!

You will practise the mission underwater. A model of the telescope will be built in a huge tank of water. You will train in the water tank. Training underwater is like working in space without gravity.

Underwater training

LIVING IN SPACE

The International Space Station (ISS) is a space laboratory.

Inside the ISS, astronauts carry out experiments. Some of the experiments are investigating how humans can survive in space.

ISS

You might be chosen for an ISS mission. You will live on the ISS for months. The space station must supply the oxygen you need to survive.

Oxygen is made using a process called electrolysis. Electricity is used to split water into hydrogen gas and oxygen gas. The electricity comes from the space station's solar panels.

Solar panels

During a mission you must eat healthily to keep strong and fit. NASA scientists will plan your meals for each day of the mission.

Many types of food are eaten in space. Some foods are dehydrated. This means all the water has been removed. To eat them you just add water to the packets.

Food has to be stored securely; otherwise it floats around due to the lack of gravity.

Your body can only survive for a few days without water. It is expensive to bring water from Earth. So, water is recycled on the ISS.

When you breathe or sweat, this produces water vapour. A machine collects the vapour and turns it back into water. Even water from your urine is recycled!

Water recycling machine

A packet of dehydrated food

Living without gravity weakens your bones and muscles. When you are living in space, you must exercise for two hours each day.

There is a treadmill and exercise bike on the ISS. The exercise will keep your muscles and bones strong. If you didn't exercise, you would not be able to stand up back on Earth!

This shuttle version of an exercise bike is called an ergometer.

Exercising on a treadmill

A harness stops
you floating around.

CHAPTER 6

SURVIVING AN EMERGENCY

Astronauts fly to and from the ISS on the space shuttle. During take-offs and landings they wear a special suit called an Advanced Crew Escape Suit.

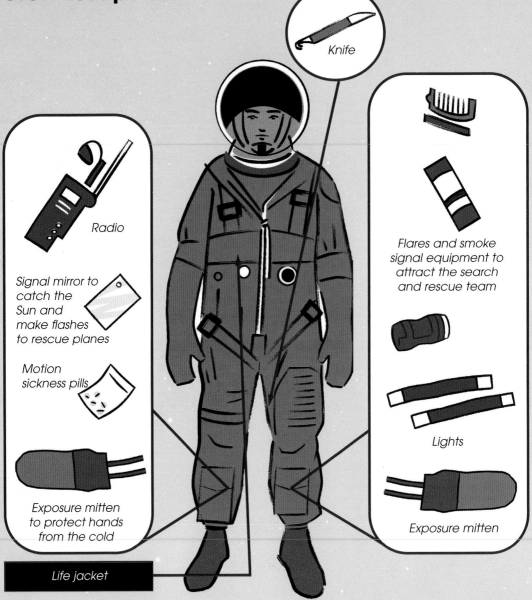

Knife

Radio

Signal mirror to catch the Sun and make flashes to rescue planes

Motion sickness pills

Exposure mitten to protect hands from the cold

Life jacket

Flares and smoke signal equipment to attract the search and rescue team

Lights

Exposure mitten

If the shuttle loses pressure, the suit will protect you. You might have to bail out over the ocean.

The suit will keep you warm. It also has lots of survival equipment.

Life jacket

Dye to turn the sea green to attract rescue planes

Device for the search and rescue team to track you by satellite

Anchor to keep the life raft in one place

One-person life raft

Cup and pump for scooping water out of the raft

carbon dioxide A gas that humans and animals breathe out. It is also produced when coal, oil and wood are burned.

crew The group of people who work on a spacecraft, aeroplane, ship or train.

environment Your surroundings.

force The scientific term for push.

garment A piece of clothing.

gravity The force that holds us onto the Earth.

Hubble Space Telescope A telescope that orbits the Earth and sends back images from outside of the Earth's solar system.

International Space Station (ISS) A space laboratory that has been built by the United States, Canada, Russia, Japan and several European countries.

laboratory A room or building where scientific experiments are carried out.

life support Something that keeps a body alive.

NASA The National Aeronautics and Space Administration is an organization in the United States that looks after US space travel and study.

primary First or most important.

solar panel A piece of equipment that uses the Sun's power to produce electricity.

water vapour A mass of tiny water droplets that look like mist.